Podcasting Made Simple

A Step-by-Step Guide to Podcasting Success

By
Hilda Labrada Gore & Charlie Birney

Eaton Press

EatonPress.com

Table of Contents

Introduction

He walked into the fluorescent-lit conference room with a box of greasy pizza and a two-liter bottle of soda. Somewhat disheveled, Charlie Birney apologized and then proceeded to warmly welcome the gathered group to the Bethesda Podcasting Meetup. This was Holistic Hilda's first encounter with Podcast Charlie. It was 2016, and Hilda had just launched her *Wise Traditions* podcast. Although she was no fan of fast food (her show is about ancestral health, after all), she was an enthusiastic podcast rookie, eager to learn from her fellow podcasters and especially from Charlie. He had a studio, gear, and know-how. Charlie was a veteran podcaster with dozens of notches on his podcast belt. He had created podcasts for those working at the coworking space Launch Workplaces in Gaithersburg, Maryland, as part of a rental deal he had brokered.

Hilda soon discovered that Charlie was as generous with his knowledge as he was with his pizza and pop. They began connecting at the Podcast Village studio, week after week. Over the course of the next few months, Hilda learned a *lot* about how to produce a show, while Charlie learned that bacon could be health food.

Along the way, Hilda gained experience, and her show was becoming increasingly popular (hitting one million downloads by the two-year mark). One day, it struck her that she and Charlie had unique skill sets that, together, could help other podcasters go from zero to sixty mph. Charlie could shed light on the tech side; he has a knack for translating complicated recording jargon into plain English. And Hilda could use her creativity and communication chops to break down the podcasting process into manageable pieces. And lest you think they've been in the media field forever, that is not the case. For decades, Charlie was a real estate developer, among other things, and played banjo in a local band as a side gig. Hilda was a translator for Interpol for a time and later a music leader for a number of area churches. Charlie and Hilda both stumbled into podcasting not because they had a "leg up" in the broadcasting field, but because they were curious, eager to have fun, and interested in conveying messages through this new medium.

If you've picked up this book, you are probably in the same boat. You've got a story you are longing to tell. You've got a message to bring and the passion to make it happen. Podcast Charlie and Holistic Hilda are here to help. Charlie brings his technical expertise and charming illustrations to most chapters; Hilda tells stories and gives insights from the trenches. Their goal? To get you podcasting by showing how easy it is to get going and giving you the confidence to take the plunge. By the time you're done reading this book, you will have a step-by-step plan for everything you need to launch your show.

Despite all the hype surrounding podcasting, you really don't need a YouTube tutorial, webinar, or expensive subscription program to get rolling. Hilda and Charlie streamline and demystify the process of podcasting in this slender tome. They keep it straightforward and accessible. You'll learn about the hardware (gear, mics, etc.) and the "software" (communication skills, chemistry, etc.) to help you launch your podcast and do so successfully. So let's get going; the world awaits your voice! Pull up a chair, grab this book (and pizza and soda, if you must), and get ready to get podcasting…fast!

1
Message:

What Do You Want to Tell the World?

Hilda

There is something inside each of us that we want to get out. We speak, text, post on social media, and even sing and move with one end in mind: to communicate. For millennia, people have used a variety of tools to get their messages across—from storytelling to songs to drawings and dance.

If a podcaster falls in the forest, will she get any listens?

Today, there are more platforms than ever for effective communication, including art (sculpture, painting, plays, music), writing (books, blog posts, articles), video (movies, YouTube clips), and the spoken word (poetry, prose). Podcasting is a unique tool that will literally amplify your voice and message to the world. You are exploring its usefulness for your message. Fantastic! Your timing couldn't be better.

A podcast is information that is "pod" ("portable on demand") and "cast" (broadcast) to the world. If you choose to use this medium, get ready for the ride of your life. Rather than waiting for some radio host to invite you on to his or her program, which will be aired at a certain time and then evaporate, now you are in control. You create the content. You push it out, and you can promote it whenever you like. It is information available on demand for you, the creator, and for the consumer—sent on your timeline and received at the listener's convenience. And the good news is that your message is likely to be "evergreen." It does not have an expiration date. It will not become dated and old (depending on the topic, of course).

There is so much to talk about, but first we want to welcome you to this wild world of podcasting. It is going to take a lot of work, but it's also going to be engaging and exciting—for you and your audience. As you set off on this adventure, we are here to help you chart your course. In a nutshell, this book will explain how to go about making digital recordings available for downloading to a computer or mobile device. (This is the very definition of the word "podcasting," by the way.) And we will explain the secret sauce to success: podcasting in such a way that the listening audience can be entertained, informed, or both. As we prepare to launch into what it takes, you must first answer a basic question.

What is your message? What are you trying to communicate? Your answer determines your direction, which is why you need clarity on this right from the start. Stephen Covey, author of *The 7 Habits of Highly Effective People*, said, "Begin with the end in mind." If you have a bunch of pieces of wood, for example, you need to decide *before* you put them together whether you're building a boat or a tree house. The same materials can construct either one. So you need to decide what you want.

Remember that the message has to be something that matters to you. You must be passionate about the topic to want to communicate it. Podcasting is simple, but it is also going to take an investment of time and commitment—a good deal of both, actually. You can't just snap your fingers and have a show appear overnight. You've got to have passion behind it so that you can persevere when challenges arise. The dictionary defines passion as a "strong and barely controllable emotion." You are going to need that drive to keep you focused and effective.

Have you ever seen an actor, performer, or politician "phoning it in?" You've picked up on the fact that they don't really believe what they're saying.

They're ambivalent about their message, and those watching begin to feel the same way. Make sure you're talking about a message that matters. It has to matter to you at least, or it won't matter to the audience.

There are shows about data, numbers, and statistics. If you asked me, Hilda, to talk about those subjects, my eyes would glaze over and my mind would hurry elsewhere. I'd have to say, "No, thank you." But I guarantee that if you are truly passionate about numbers, call your podcast *Mathlete*, and happily geek out about such topics, you will find a listening audience of like-minded souls who will tune in.

By the way, don't worry that someone else has already covered your topic. If you quickly go through Apple's list of podcasts and there are ten, twenty, or more shows about your passion, that's OK! What if pop artists refused to sing a song about love or heartbreak because someone else had already sung a song like that? You guessed it: They'd be out of work, but by their own choice.

Any topic can strike an emotional chord with the audience when hit from a fresh angle. Don't "x" yourself out at the starting line. Consider the example of the singer: No one else is singing that particular song with his or her unique voice. So use your voice, go with what you love, and get it out there. There is no other *you* out there; this much we know for certain.

Determine your message

Step one, therefore, is to determine what your

"What do you call a podcaster with an audience of one?"
"Successful!"

message is because it will help you select the best method to convey it. If you want to launch a fan show focused on a Netflix series, for example, you might want to have a co-host to bounce around theories about the direction of the plot or character development. If you're going to have a show about meditation because you know the world needs more quiet and contemplation, you're probably going to do a solo show (just you and the mic), with quiet music in the background.

As you consider what you want to communicate, keep in mind what will happen next. You are not only getting a message out, but you are also making a space for connection. What you launch will create a community. What will that look like? What will best serve your listeners? Sticking with the two illustrations above, a fan show is meant to allow for delving into the characters and plot on a series you love. You want to go beyond watching. You want to interact with others who obsess about the show as much as you do. And your podcast will start to create a community where all of you can connect.

The same goes for a meditation program. Even though it is typically seen as a solitary endeavor of introspection and mindfulness, listeners will be eager to connect with one another to discuss experiences, share techniques, and the like. Your show will create a new space for people to engage with one another.

Think of your local coffee shop: Coffee is its product, but it is about much more than that. The best shops are creating places of community where all are welcome to exchange ideas and build relationships.

Connect to the listener

Once you've considered what you want to communicate (primary message/topic) and what you will create (community) around the show, you will need to give some thought to the people you are communicating *to* and connecting *with*. This matters because podcasting is a two-way street. It might seem like a one-way relationship where you broadcast your thoughts, but it is much more than this. Hopefully, you are not getting on the air just to make money (because if you are, I hope you are a patient person—it might take a looooong while)! Chances are what you really want is to get something out from inside you and share it with the world. "Share" is the operative word. A gift is useless if it is given but left unwrapped and untouched. You are not communicating and creating a product for yourself. You want to make a genuine impact.

What I want you to do at this stage is envision your "audience avatar." Who is your target audience? What are their lives like? Start to picture the individuals who will likely listen to your show. This exercise will help you shape your message to make the greatest impact. For example, let's say you are a podcaster who wants to talk about how to nurture wellness. It so happens I have a show about this! I need to consider who I'm talking to. Is my avatar listener a couch potato? Or a person who is already a "foodie" but wants to up his or her game and find locally sourced alpaca meat? Big difference, right?

As you consider your "avatar listener," consider his or her approximate age and stage in life, interests, hopes and aspirations, and current lifestyle. You can even name the person, in your mind. By getting this specific, you can imagine that you are speaking directly to that person when you are recording an episode. And you can also keep this avatar in mind throughout your whole podcast development process: when you choose the title of the episode, what you emphasize as you promote it, etc. The avatar helps you focus so that you achieve the goal of connecting with and meeting the needs of your listener.

I watched a comedian bomb one time. His jokes were not hitting home, and the whole crowd could feel it. It might simply have been a case of not knowing his audience. That's probably why the connection wasn't made. Jokes designed to make middle-school boys laugh will fall flat to an audience of their moms. This is what we're trying to avoid.

> Your message is what you COMMUNICATE
> Your audience will be the COMMUNITY
> that grows around the topic
> You will foster a genuine CONNECTION
> when you envision who they are

At this stage, you are not choosing a message or avatar listener in order to maximize downloads. (If you were doing that, you would simply launch a podcast about sex!) Rather, you are trying to properly define your message and who you want to reach. When done thoughtfully, your show will be focused and more likely to reach a growing number of listeners. The idea is to narrow down your niche so you can be successful.

Success is not about numbers; it's about having a show that affects people the way you hope it will—fanboying together over the protagonist of the Netflix show, learning to have a meditative moment during a coffee break at work, and discovering the nourishment that comes from cheese instead of Cheetos.

2
Method:

The Best Way to Communicate Your Story

Hilda

The method you choose is intricately tied to your message. Imagine that you have built your boat. It is the message. Which direction should you sail in? This is the method. How can you best arrive at your destination (of connection and community)? As you get started on this voyage, here are some ideas about which way to go.

Solo show

This is a great medium for people who are talkers (raise your hands, podcasters—that's how most of us got into this). My elementary school report cards consistently noted that I talked too much. That weakness has now become my strength. It might be yours as well. Podcasters need to know how to fill the silences.

"I asked my shrink, 'Why do I podcast?' He said, 'Because you want to live in a fantasy world.'"

But a solo show is not just for talkers. You have to be able to entertain. Are you the type of person whom people crowd around at parties? Can you tell a good story? Do you have people laughing at your crazy illustrations or approach to life? You would be a perfect solo host.

You should also be knowledgeable. Podcasting used to be a "blue ocean"—a new platform with very little competition. (The term "blue ocean" was made popular by the book *Blue Ocean Strategy: How to Create Uncontested Market Space and Make Competition Irrelevant* by W. Chan Kim and Renee Mauborgne.) Podcasting at first was like the broad, blue ocean—wide open, with lots of room for swimming and no other fish or sharks around. You could publish your show and it would sparkle and catch the eye in the deep blue sea. There was nothing out there like it for miles around.

In contrast, today the ocean is "red," with lots of competition regardless of the topic. Your show is crowded and squished, (if not outright torn apart) by dozens of others in the same field. It's tougher to be noticed and difficult to navigate. This is one reason it is critical to be both entertaining *and* knowledgeable; this will set your show apart and have folks tuning in more frequently. Think about why people turn to comedians for news today: because they are informed, informing, *and* entertaining. Whatever you do, you must look for ways to showcase your skill set(s) so that you offer something unique to the listener.

You also have to know when to shut up. You do not want to be talking for the sake of hearing yourself speak. A podcast is not a place for people to kill time. Make sure you have something to say; otherwise, the listener will tune out and turn off the episode. Podcasting isn't just about talking; it's about knowing when the show is over. New podcasters often ask how long their show should be. Dave Jackson of *School of Podcasting* says, "Stop when you're done." But this is not as easy as it seems. Because many of us are talkers, we can go on and on about any topic. You might want to solicit honest feedback from early trial episodes to figure out where to draw the "done" line.

Writers are told that you must "kill your darlings." This means that however much you love the words on the page, it's better to be concise and succinct. (Notice the redundancy in the previous sentence. This was a test to see if you were on your toes.) So streamline your show. Trim the fat.

Do not use more words than necessary. Be careful not to become so enamored with the sound of your own voice that you go on much longer than the listener can bear.

This is something that I (Charlie) learned personally. I was the co-host and board operator for the *Jeff Miller Show* for two years. I always sent the finished episodes to Jeff and his wife for a listen and quick edit after I had done my part. Early on, until I learned how to curb my own storytelling, the usual feedback was: "Please tell Charlie to take out the story about his dog/child/fill-in-the-blank." Jeff's wife was 100 percent right! Those wonderful stories were not the right fit for his show, and I learned to share more strategically. Edit what you are saying, before you even say it. It saves time in post-production.

Caution! Speaking of sound: A raspy or monotone voice will not be well-suited to a solo show. Just saying. Your voice needs to be easy to listen to. You might want to get vocal coaching, just as singers do. Join a Toastmasters club or mastermind group where you can practice public speaking. You must learn (and master) proper breathing techniques and diction. Get objective feedback on the sound of your voice. If improving your voice doesn't seem realistic, take heart—you can still get your message out. Consider one of the other methods mentioned below or become a producer of the podcast and have someone else be the host.

Messages that work for solo shows: educational, informative, humorous.

Solo shows that work: *Smart Passive Income* (Pat Flynn), *School of Podcasting* (Dave Jackson), *Grammar Girl* (Mignon Fogarty), *The Story Behind* (Emily Prokop)

"Who is the podcaster's best and only friend?" "Mike" (mic).

Co-hosting show

Glenn Hebert, featured in the documentary on podcasting titled *The Messengers*, says you should only co-host with someone who is a true friend or who you'd be willing to go on a long road trip with. Co-hosting is different from interviewing guests (who rotate in and out of your life). A co-host is a person who has equal time behind the mic with you. Glenn is right in the sense that you really need to get along. Chemistry can't be faked. Nicole Kidman and Tom Cruise starred in *Eyes Wide Shut* together, and even though they were lovers in real life, the chemistry did not translate to the big screen. So not only can chemistry not be faked, even if you think it's there, it simply might not translate to the medium.

Successful co-hosting depends on chemistry, timing, relationship, and sound—a mix of factors that can be hard to quantify so you are definitely going to have to experiment to see if this works for you. And don't just co-host with a friend and then pat yourselves on the back that you did it. You have to record an episode (or two or three) and invite people to honestly tell you if they feel it's working or not. If you enjoy each other, that's great, but it's not enough. You need to make sure the audience enjoys you, too.

The same principles I wrote for the solo host hold true for co-hosts. You need to entertain, be knowledgeable, and know when to shut up. In addition to those guidelines, you will need to develop the following skills.

- **Listen to each other and sample your sound.** Interrupting or speaking over each other (unless a part of the purposeful, playful banter) is difficult on the listener and annoying. You must be able to take turns speaking so that your voices can be distinct and understood clearly.

"How are podcasters and fishermen alike?"
"They both lie about how big theirs is."

- **Play off each other.** Carrie Underwood and Brad Paisley have co-hosted the Country Music Association Awards ten years in a row. Why are they invited back year after year? Because they know how to interact and amuse each other and the audience. If you can do this

"Do you listen to podcasts?" "Um...I have a Squarespace website, wear MeUndies, use ZipRecruiter, and sleep on a Casper mattress. Any other questions?"

naturally with your co-host, that is awesome. Otherwise, study how the pros do it and seek to develop that playful interaction piece.

- **Disagree with each other.** Film critics Gene Siskel and Roger Ebert had a tremendously popular TV show that lasted almost a couple of decades. The secret to their longevity? That back-and-forth banter, yes, but also their differences of opinion. Movie aficionados (like sports fans) love to hear more than one opinion, and the more heated the argument, the more fun.

- **Lean into each other's strengths.** You are bound to have different strengths than your co-host. This is awesome. It will help your audience know who's talking (especially if you are the same gender) if one of you is responsible for a particular segment of the show. Use effects or the same lead each time to demarcate the sections that spotlight you as individuals. On the *She Podcasts* show, Elsie Escobar and Jessica Kupferman do this very well. Elsie has the "Elsie's Tool Tips" segment, in which she talks about the latest app or gizmo for producing or marketing your show, and Jessica has the "News You Can Use" piece, which highlights news that affects the podcasting community.

Caution! Some people enjoy their co-host so much that they spend far too much time on what they consider playful banter, but that delays the start of the actual content. Be careful to give listeners what they want. If they are listening because they want that banter alone, great. Stick with it. But if you are promising something else, don't waste their time discussing how drunk you got over the weekend. If you don't know where to draw the line, invite honest feedback to find out where it should be.

Messages that work for co-hosting shows: comedy, sports, informational, educational

Co-hosting shows that work: *2 Dope Queens* (Phoebe Robinson and Jessica Williams), *Podcasters' Roundtable* (Ray Ortega, Dave Jackson, Daniel J. Lewis), *She Podcasts* (Jessica Kupferman and Elsie Escobar).

Interview format

Having guests on a show is a great way to create an engaging podcast. The pressure is off to entertain and engage because you have someone to carry the conversation. To make this work, you need to identify potential guests. Where to begin? Find influencers, authors, or speakers in your field and start to follow them on social media and in real life (when possible, but not in a stalker-type way). They will recognize your name from comments on their posts and will get to know you. Should you attend the same conference or festival, try to connect with them socially at a preconference mixer or party. The more connected you are before the "ask," the more likely you will get a "yes" to the invitation to be on your show.

When pursuing guests, start with low-hanging fruit such as friends of friends or people with a modest following or influence (you're probably in that same category anyway). Excellent guests will be entertaining and informative; it doesn't really matter how well-known they are—at first.

Do you want to get the big fish, though? Be on the lookout for experts in the field, folks featured on other podcasts, bloggers, TV or radio personalities, etc. Follow the advice listed above, but do note: The bigger they are, the harder they will be to get, so make it easy for them to say yes. Get a mutual friend to introduce you or recommend your show. Once you have contact information, follow through via a scheduling app for your interviews, such as Calendly, Acuity Scheduling, or Schedule Once. Whatever you do, be professional, and once they set the date, lock it in. Tell them what to expect (how long it will take, whether it is an audio or video show, whether they should have a mic on their end, etc.).

Be the best listener! Most important, when you have a guest on the show, make sure to listen. A good interview is essentially a conversation that is a sincere back-and-forth. When you listen, you will become curious, and questions will naturally come to mind. If asking questions off the cuff makes you nervous, write some down ahead of time. You can even make a list of simple questions that will work for every guest, based on the questions reporters ask:

- Who? (Tell me about yourself.)

- What (do you know that I don't)?

- When (did you learn it)?

- Where (in the world is this applied)?

- Why (is it important)?

- How (can we live this out, too)?

"What's the quickest way to a podcaster's heart?"
"An iTunes review."

To structure a deeper interview, study how others do it. And try to create something of a story arc. On my (Hilda's) Wise Traditions podcast, I like to start with the problem (focus on a particular sickness/disease), look at the solution (how it can be overcome), and discuss applications to our own lives (how the listener can get there, too). Movies and books are structured similarly.

Also, when conducting interviews, I've found that it's important to ask a skeptical question or two because some listeners will certainly be asking themselves those very questions. I like to make these more palatable by putting the words in someone else's mouth—e.g., "What would you say to the person who finds this hard to swallow?" Or "Some people would say you're off the wall. What would you tell them?"

Caution! Some experts will do a series of podcasts on one subject when they release a book or get some new exposure. Beware of asking the guest the same questions everyone else asks. This will be boring for them and won't reveal anything new to those who follow the speaker/author. It's best if you can find something unique about him or her by doing some research and digging around online.

And speaking of digging around, you must do some homework when inviting guests to be on your show. You have to be prepared to ask intelligent, probing questions. At the very least, read the guest's bio online and a recent article or two from his or her website. It's sweet if you can have an intern do these things for you and then give you a summary or starter questions, but for now, you will need to do the prep work yourself.

Messages that work for interview shows: Educational (where experts are the heavyweights and you are the one tapping into what they know) on just about any topic: fitness, health, money, acting, nature, etc. Entertainment, information, fandom of a particular series or genre of media.

Interview shows that work: *How I Built This* (Guy Raz), *Wise Traditions* (Hilda Labrada Gore), *Little Known Facts* (Ilana Levine)

Storytelling

These shows are riveting because humans are hard-wired for storytelling. Traditional cultures were oral cultures—passing down true stories, myths, history, and lore. People are captivated by stories, whether they are told in person or via movies, books, radio, or podcasts. This is probably the most labor-intensive podcast format of the bunch. To properly launch a storytelling podcast, you will need:

- **Music.** Many podcasts use music clips as part of the intro and outro, as a type of brand for the show's feel, transitions, etc. But you might also need music to set the mood or add tension.

- **Solid vocal chops.** Whether it's one narrator or several actors, vocal quality is critical. No one wants to listen to a whiny voice tell a story. (See the "Caution!" section of the solo format.) Can you vary your volume and vocal dynamics enough to keep people engaged? Practice reading aloud in front of others and ask for honest feedback.

- **A story (obviously).** What story do you want to tell? How will you find it? Are you going to write scripts yourself? Will you look for true stories or fiction that has already been published?

- **A story arc.** In each episode and over the course of a season, you need to take the listener on a journey. This is critical. Why should people stay tuned? They need to be invested in the characters and curious about the outcome. Just like a story on the written page, a podcast must have character development and progress with the plot. If these are not present, your audience will not be present either.

Caution! This genre seems to be the most work to me. You can't wing it and hope the guest will be entertaining with extemporaneous speaking. You really need to have your scripts in order before beginning to record, especially if the material is original. I would suggest running your scripts and/or season by some folks for feedback to see if they resonate before officially launching.

Messages that work for storytelling shows: True crime. *Serial* was one of the first big hits of podcasting because the story was compelling. Was Adnan guilty of the crime for which he had been convicted? Week by week, more threads and storylines were revealed—witnesses who had something to add, a question about some aspect of the alibi, etc. True crime is one of the most popular genres in the storytelling format to date.

Storytelling shows that work: *Radiolab* (Jad Abumrad and Robert Krulwich), *The Moth Radio Hour* (PRX), *Love + Radio* (Nick van der Kolk).

This list of messages and methods is not exhaustive by any means. That's the beauty of podcasting. You might come up with something that has never been done before. Fantastic! Podcasting is for creatives, certainly. Choose the method that will help you reach your audience and go for it!

3
Medium:

The Essential Gear for Podcasting

Charlie

So you know what you want to talk about and how you're going to convey your message. Let's talk about the stuff. What gear do you need to get started recording? How much will it cost to do this well and have a good, consistent sound?

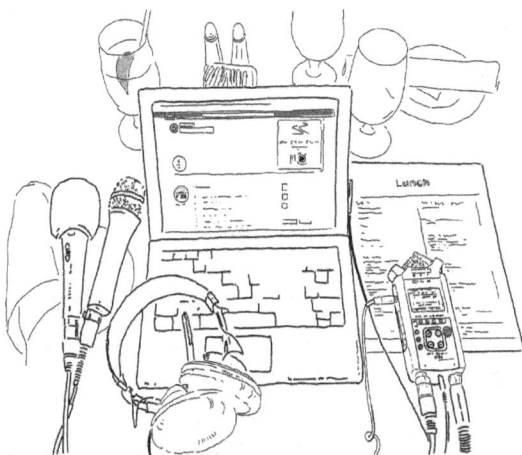

"Beware of GAS - gear acquisition syndrome!"

You might have some of the necessary items already and not realize it. Do you have a webcam on your computer? Some people use a webcam to record episodes while others mostly use their phones to capture and even edit audio. As an amateur musician, I had some microphones and XLR cables (microphone cables) in my possession already. I even had a small PA system for performances, and I really thought it could be used as a mixer. (It couldn't, but you will find that a simple mixer can be one of the most affordable pieces of equipment for your studio.) So look around your house and see what you have on hand. There's no need to make a big investment in gear just to get the ball rolling.

Here is the short list of gear for basic podcasting:

1. Microphone.

The mic takes the sound waves from your voice and converts them into electrical energy (so that they can be captured). There are many micro-phones on the market to choose from. My first and most dependable mics were the Shure SM57s (less

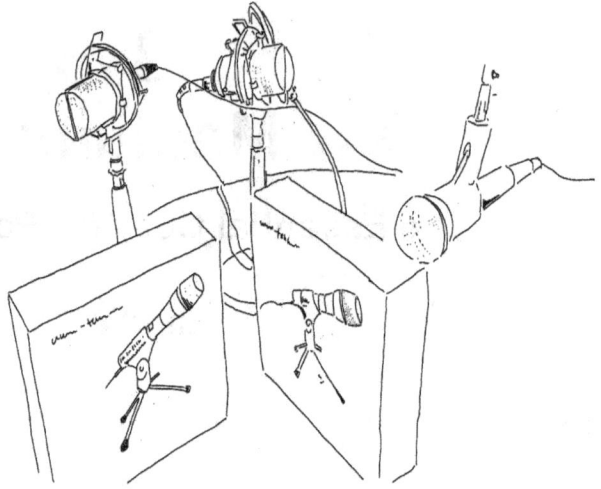

Cinco de microphone

than $100 each). The microphones send the signals to the...

2. Audio mixer.
A mixer takes all the electrical signals it receives and mixes them together into one (or more) output signals. It's like baking a cake: Your voice, music, effects, etc., are the ingredients that are poured, mixed together, and converted into one final (and tasty) product. The mixer (aka "the board") produces that product: the output signal. Phys-ically, it is a box or device that you plug your microphone cables and digital recorder into. Speaking of which, the mixer is connected (via a cable or cord) to the...

3. Digital recorder.
This device actually records the inputs. It's the place the cake is "baked," if you will. In the old days, we would press "record" and capture audio on cassette tape or film. Now we record sound digitally. The signals are converted into numbers and kept on a little card for safekeeping, so we can store or transfer the recorded information/file at will. And when you are ready to taste the cake, you will need...

4. Headphones/earphones.
OK, this is where the illustration breaks down. You can't taste with your ears. Or can you? You need to sample your sound, after all. What does the show sound like? Can you hear yourself? Your guest? Headphones/earphones are like little speakers

placed next to or in your ears. They give you an idea of what your final product sounds like.

That's it. (I told you it was a short list!) You will definitely need a computer later, but you probably already have one of those. At this point, we are just talking about capturing your sounds. In fact, you might decide down the line to stick to interviewing and recording and have someone else do the editing. If that's the case, you might not need a computer at all.

However, if you are a technophile or someone who wants the ultimate in sound quality, here are some ideas for going above and beyond the bare-bones start-up equipment and achieving a more professional podcasting sound:

1. **Additional microphones** (two or more)
2. **Foam filters** (aka "cough filters") for each microphone
3. **Cables/cords** for each microphone and to run from the mixer to your digital recorder. Sometimes XLR cables are required; other times 1/4-inch cables are needed. Look at your devices to see what fits.
4. **Multi-channel audio mixer** allows you to record multiple voices at once; make sure you have a mixer (or board) with four channels
5. **Power supply** so you are ready to record anywhere/anytime
6. **Extension cord**
7. **Deluxe headphones** for discerning nuances of sounds and effects
8. **Digital recorder.**

The higher the quality of the recorder, the more likely you are to get the best possible results. And don't forget that a laptop or even a smartphone can record your sound.

9. **Spare batteries** for said digital recorder

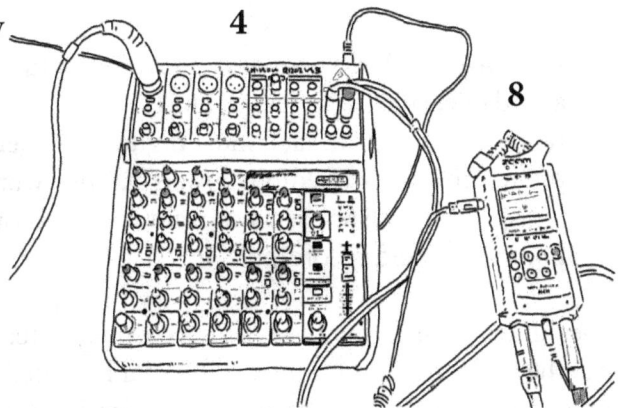

10. SD card and a spare for storage options

When you want more than one person to hear what is being recorded (which you do), invest in a headphone amplifier and headphones for each guest.

Let's take a deeper dive into the gear and try to understand a little more of what is going on here.

- **Audio mixer.** What does the mixing board do? You are trying to make the voices even and easy to listen to. The board takes one or more inputs and lets you try to balance them with each other. You have several ways to control and shape the sound using the "gain" and "level" knobs (which we explain in Chapter 6). For now, you just need to know that there are all shapes, sizes, and costs of mixing boards, but your first one can easily cost less than $100, especially if it only has one or two channels.

- **Effects and equalizer.** Most mixers have a few effects built into the board, including some equalizer levels. You can experiment to try to take a voice that is very low or very high and soften the sound a little. Typically, I do not play with the equalizer very much, but it can come in handy in some situations. The key is to experiment. You are creating an experience for the ear, and you want it to sound as clean, crisp, and listener-friendly as possible. And don't forget to listen to it yourself afterward to see if it passes the test.

- **Digital recorder.** These devices are really fun. They are often affordable, starting at less than $100 each, and have an amazing range of abilities. In fact, most digital recorders have built-in microphones that are incredibly powerful. They work well in your recording space and also when you want to record outside your studio or home (aka field recording).

Speaking of which, here is a field-recording note: It is tempting to use the built-in microphone on a digital recorder for field work. That might work very well in certain situations, but for others, it might not. The problem is that the built-in microphone might not distinguish the sound of your voice from the ambient noise (crowds, dogs barking, ambulances passing by, etc.), and you could end up with an audio mess.

So when you plan on recording outside your normal studio, you should experiment with an external mic plugged into the digital recorder. In this case, you will not have a mixer. Experiment with setting the levels on the recorder and with using the automatic level control

R2D2 has yet another message he wants to get across.

that is probably built into the device. Remember: In this setting you are only able to balance the input level for all incoming audio, so the microphone technique—how far you and the other voices are from the mic—becomes very important. Tell everyone to try to stay in the same general area in relation to the mic once you hit "record."

You are simply trying to get the best elements to make the best sound in the setting where the discussion/interview takes place. I have deliberately kept the lists limited to help you avoid GAS (gear acquisition syndrome). There are lots of fancy-schmancy microphones and gadgets that people will tell you are a "must" for podcasting. But don't buy it. The basics will suffice, especially in the beginning.

4
Practice:

Learn From Our Mistakes (and Successes)

Hilda & Charlie

Every school kid knows that practice is critical when it comes to learning something new—be it a sport or a musical instrument. You pick up the ball. You grab the violin bow. You get going. You have to start somewhere. It's not pretty (especially not at first when you are learning to play the violin), but if you stick with it, you can get pretty good and start to garner an audience. Once you have your message, your method, and your equipment, you need to shift into gear and get going. It's time to practice.

To set the stage for you, here are our stories. We want to give you a quick look at what we learned as we got rolling and through fits and starts along the way. You'll see the solid steps and the missteps, and hopefully learn from both.

Hilda's Story: How Tears Watered the Seed of My Podcasting Career
I was a blogger and all about writing. I had been writing for some seven years about my personal life and faith. The theme was general encouragement. I didn't have an avatar reader, so I wasn't very focused. I just wanted to inspire people. My blog site was squarepegbeliever.com. (You can go there and read my old posts, if you dare!) I was not branded well, obviously. This blog had absolutely nothing to do with the television show *Square Pegs*. I was trying to communicate that I was unique through the title, but so what? Everybody else is, too. Although I enjoyed the practice of writing, I struggled to grow an audience (no surprise here).

I became a health coach through the Institute for Integrative Nutrition in 2013. I wanted to rebrand, thank goodness. So I switched the name of my blog to chispablog.wordpress.com. I know. From bad to worse, right? I named my fledgling company Chispa, which means "spark" in Spanish and had been my nickname in the past. My tag line was "sparking a healthier you." Cute, but who was I trying to make healthier? I had no idea. But I was moving and trying to get the hang of what my audience wanted and needed. I was a bit more focused in my writing, and I got a little bit more of a following.

The turning point that nudged me from blogging to podcasting was when a reader and friend sent me a message via Facebook telling me to call her about one of my posts. This friend lived in Nashville and worked for a publishing house, so I'm not lying when I tell you that I was kind of excited and hopeful. Was a potential book deal in the works? Was I being discovered? When I called, I found out that what she wanted to tell me was that my last blog post was horrible and unhelpful. I had written about sugar addiction and how to wean yourself from it. I was not speaking from experience, so I think that is one reason I was "off the mark."

She, on the other hand, had struggled with sugar in her diet and weight issues her entire life. She was offended and found my suggestions irritating. As we spoke, she told me that an author should write as 1) a sage/expert, 2) a fellow struggler, or 3) a signpost/guide. She suggested (gently) that I was far from a sage in her opinion or a fellow struggler. This being the case, she recommended that I be a signpost, that I seek out the sages and interview them. She even said that I should start a podcast.

I hung up the phone and burst into tears. I am not a crier, but it was hard to hear that my post had disappointed her and that it hadn't resonated. But on another level, I was grateful for her honesty. I heard her, and a seed was planted (though it was indeed watered by my tears).

I had my subject: health. But I still had to figure out how to get my message out there. In the summer of 2015, I took a trip to Kenya as a representative of the Weston A. Price Foundation, an ancestral health

nutrition group (westonaprice.
org). They sent me as a volunteer
to speak to people in Nairobi and a
remote Maasai tribe in Oiti. What a
wild and exciting turn of events—
that I could travel and speak about
wellness and the importance of
traditional, real foods! While there,
things got even wilder when I
found an opportunity to be interviewed on a radio program. The
power and reach of broadcasting
made a huge impression on me.
The thought crossed my mind in
the studio in Nairobi: If I could be
on the radio in Kenya, why not in
the U.S.?

"I've been thinking about stopping a podcast…
said no one ever."

The final spark that catapulted me into podcasting occurred that fall
when I returned to the U.S. A fifteen-year-old boy in my church band
said he was starting a podcast. The moment he uttered those words,
my next thought was: "If *he* can start a podcast, *I* can start a podcast." It
struck me that it could not be that hard if he was going for it.

So the dream began taking shape. I mentioned the idea of starting a
show to my family. One of my daughter's friends, Jane, told me that she
was aiming to launch a podcast about the process of becoming a nurse.
She got me a copy of John Lee Dumas' book, *Podcast Launch*. And the
deal was sealed. This would become my podcast primer. I read it cover
to cover and then put what the author wrote into action. I still hadn't
listened to a podcast besides *Serial*, and I didn't have any podcasting
peers. So I was flying blind when I walked into Best Buy to buy my first
microphone (one that would connect to the USB port in my laptop).

To get the experts to interview was my next step. I didn't know a soul in
serious nutrition/wellness circles. But I was a volunteer chapter leader
for the nutrition group that had sent me to Kenya, so I approached the
organization's leaders with a proposal to start a podcast. I knew they

had a vast network of authors and speakers whose articles they published in their quarterly journal and who spoke at their annual conference. I also knew that they had 11,000 members so I figured that if I launched a show on their behalf, there would be great potential for an audience of avid listeners.

Happily, they agreed. We signed a contract in November 2015. I attended their conference and began interviewing guests. I launched the Wise Traditions podcast in January 2016, with tech help from my husband. In January 2018, we reached the one million download mark, with episodes averaging between 10,000 and 30,000 listens.

Does it sound a bit too much like it was a breeze? Well, it wasn't that easy. It certainly wasn't all peaches and cream. Here are a few of my podcasting missteps:

1. Whiff. My first interview was a test. I set it up with farmer Jesse Straight from Whiffletree Farm. I wanted to be ready for the conference in November, when I would be interviewing *lots* of speakers. So I met Jesse in D.C. while he was making farm-food deliveries. I had practiced at home with my equipment ahead of time, so I felt ready. But when I got back from the interview and attempted to listen to my audio…crickets. No, it wasn't actually crickets. It was one long screeching sound. I was appalled, broken-hearted, and devastated. I had evidently pushed the wrong button. It was such a good interview, and it was lost forever!

2. Sounds like. My first mic was a Rode (not condenser) mic. My first software: Audio Hijack. Editing software: Fission. It was all serviceable, but as I honed my recording skills, I found myself less and less happy with the sound and editing options at my fingertips. (According to some early listener feedback, the show sounded like I was recording in an echoey bathroom!) But at least I was practicing, right? It's like playing t-ball rather than baseball—you've got to start somewhere.

3. Sponsored by…. I thought the nutrition group would have no trouble finding sponsors to cover the podcast initiative. After all, it had a quarterly journal that had many, many advertisers in the back of each issue. I was wrong. Dead wrong. The advertisers had no idea what a podcast was, so they didn't sign up for a long time. Even now, two years later, we have to actively recruit them and offer discounted prices for advertising on the show rather than follow the CPM model (cost per mille/thousand listeners) that is currently the industry standard. We even launched a Patreon account to garner support. Two people sponsored the show, to the tune of $10 per month.

4. No Picasso. The show's original artwork was subpar. We needed to decide quickly because the show was going to launch in two months, so we

"Glad we got out of jail yesterday." "Yup, me, too. We sure were in a heap of treble."

settled on a picture of a healthy little boy who was in the water. The problem was that it gave the impression that the show was about children or swimming lessons or something. (Thank goodness, we finally changed it!)

Practice is about trying and sometimes failing. Practice is what you do when you want to improve. So go ahead and experiment. Like Charlie and I, you are bound to have some successes and some colossal mistakes. It's OK. None of the mistakes are insurmountable, and they will all contribute to your ultimate success.

Charlie's Story: Launching Podcasts...and Podcast Village

I started out as a listener and, like Hilda, an amateur musician. When the idea struck to create a podcast, I naively thought that I was already set. I had all the equipment. I could use my PA system mixer for the podcast. (I couldn't.) I had microphones. (They were the wrong kind, and I had only two.) I was a musician, so I knew how to handle a microphone and maybe interview a guest, right? None of that really worked out the way I thought it would, but it got me started.

Once I figured out what I really needed, a simple four-track Behringer mixing board was my first purchase. I already had an Edirol digital recorder that I rarely used for music.

I was doing non-podcast-related business and had moved into a coworking space in Gaithersburg, Maryland, called Launch Workplaces. Coworking was a new concept to me (I used to be a property manager and leasing agent), but it made sense.

But what does this mean for my podcast journey? At Launch Workplaces, every door and every desk represented a different story: talent agents, video instruction, marketing agencies, home lighting, financial management, business strategies, the local technology council, a high school robotics team, furniture movers, real estate agents—the list went on and on.

As a Launch tenant and a resident of Montgomery County, I was asked by the crew at Launch to do what I could to introduce people to their new coworking space. Then I ran into my friend Jeff Davis, who was doing some public relations for Launch Workplaces.

Jeff and I were avid podcast listeners (*For Immediate Release* with Shel Holtz is probably our favorite). We had done a few really fun social media promotions in the past—like using QR codes on tee signs for the sponsors of a golf tournament. (I think we might have been a little ahead of our time with that one!) However, the idea to try a

"I love your podcast! I just watched it."

podcast as a way of promoting the space bubbled up in both our minds: Let's do a coworking show and call it *Launch Podcast*.

And without really knowing what we were doing, that is exactly
what we did. The idea was pretty simple: Each week, we interviewed
someone in or around Launch Workplaces. That was it. They could give
their best elevator speech, and then if they wanted, they could post the
show to their website, LinkedIn profile (very popular), Facebook page,
or newsletter. Launch Workplaces uses the podcast in all its media. And
to date, it is the only coworking space with a built-in podcast studio.

But to go back to our very first interview, I have to fess up to one of my
missteps. Jeff and I had two microphones and one guest, so you do the
math. Three people, two mics. With no microphone in front of me, I
sounded like I was recording from a very distant country. It was pretty
unprofessional. For some reason, I thought it would all sound OK, but
I thought wrong. (If you are really curious, give a listen and judge for
yourself: soundcloud.com/launch-podcast/launch-podcast-ware-acad-
emy-121214-1004-pm?in=launch-podcast/sets/launch-podcasts. You
will need to jump past the first few minutes to hear what I am talking
about. You can even see the mistake in the waveform.)

But it worked, even without a third microphone. We had our first
episode under our belt. I went out and got a few more mics. (And then
a new board and some more headphones and another digital recorder
and business cards, and….)

From there, it just seemed to grow. Jeff and I thought, "Why stop at just
one podcast show? We have the gear—let's do one about social media!"
(soundcloud.com/launch-podcast/sets/practically-social)

Immediately, we started to see that the Launch Workplaces guests
might want their own podcast series—and they did.

I made a lot of mistakes the first year, but I also learned a lot about the
mechanics of recording (and posting, producing show art, marketing,
etc.). And now, all these years later, I am the founder of Podcast Village,
a group that trains podcasters, produces shows, and promotes them. It's
a tribute to the benefits of practice.

5
Prep:
Indispensable Steps and Strategies for an Effective Launch

Hilda & Charlie

Some of you might be researchers, eager to learn more about stats and strategies as you prepare to launch. Others, the doers among you, might want more specifics about how to launch. We will address all of the above in this section. As of publication time, these are the latest industry stats from Edison Research.

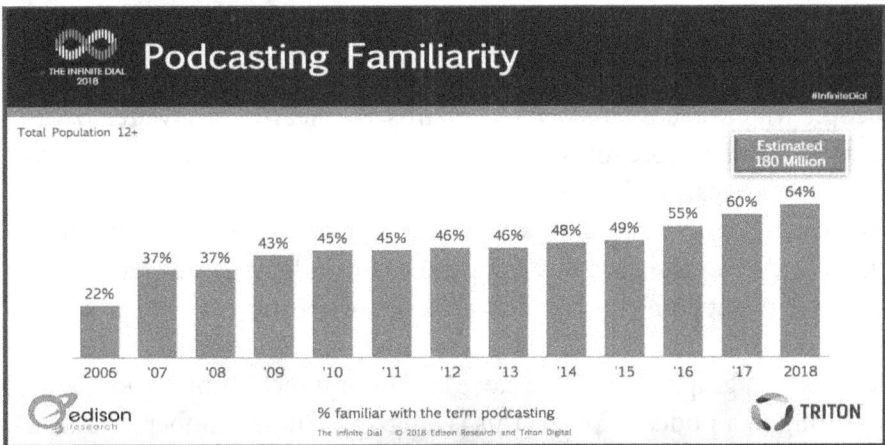

Podcasting Familiarity — Total Population 12+ — % familiar with the term podcasting. 2006: 22%, '07: 37%, '08: 37%, '09: 43%, '10: 45%, '11: 45%, '12: 46%, '13: 46%, '14: 48%, '15: 49%, '16: 55%, '17: 60%, 2018: 64%. Estimated 180 Million.

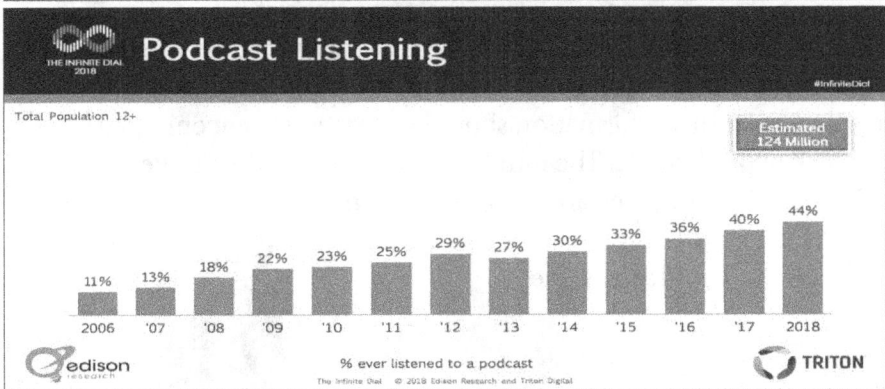

Podcast Listening — Total Population 12+ — % ever listened to a podcast. 2006: 11%, '07: 13%, '08: 18%, '09: 22%, '10: 23%, '11: 25%, '12: 29%, '13: 27%, '14: 30%, '15: 33%, '16: 36%, '17: 40%, 2018: 44%. Estimated 124 Million.

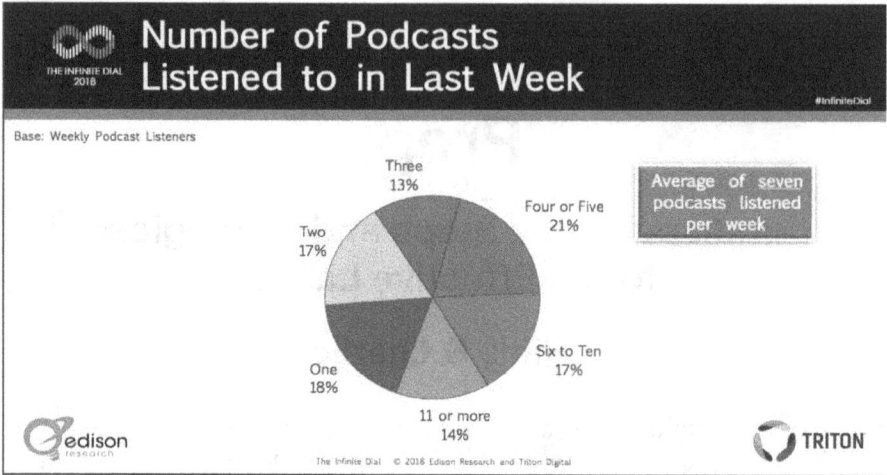

Number of Podcasts Listened to in Last Week

Base: Weekly Podcast Listeners

Three 13%
Four or Five 21%
Two 17%
One 18%
Six to Ten 17%
11 or more 14%

Average of seven podcasts listened per week

edison research

TRITON

The Infinite Dial © 2018 Edison Research and Triton Digital

You can find the most current report by searching at "The Infinite Dial" link: www.edisonresearch.com/infinite-dial-2018.

Stats

Let's break down the graphs. The first one indicates the number of people who are familiar with podcasting. It's clearly an upward trajectory. More and more folks are familiar with what a podcast is. This is important because if people don't know what a podcast is, there is absolutely no way they could possibly listen. How can you buy a product if you've never even heard of it? But if they are at least somewhat familiar with the term, you have a fighting chance of getting in their earbuds.

The second graph shows that close to half of the U.S. population is listening to a podcast. Wow! This is amazing. These numbers are also going up. The more people listen, the more likely it is that they will listen to you. And the third graph demonstrates that once people start listening, they don't just listen to one show. Most listen to multiple podcasts. All this information should be extremely encouraging. The trends are predictable. The numbers are going up, up, up! People know what podcasts are, they are listening, and they are tuning in to multiple shows. Podcasting is on the rise. And you are producing one of the shows that can ride the wave.

Strategies
Here are some of our best practices to help you ride that wave well.

- **Build excitement before launching.** Let your potential listeners know what you are doing. Go to them for advice on picking artwork. Start networking and advertising wherever your audience is.

- **When you launch, have several episodes ready to go right out of the gate.** If you launch with only one episode, it not only looks lonely on Apple Podcasts, but it gives the impression that not much is going on. Think of a store's grand opening. You want to have buzz, excitement, and products on the shelves.

- **Plan ahead.** You have to set yourself up for success and avoid the dreaded "podfade." After thirteen or fourteen episodes, some podcasters lose steam and stop producing their shows. Newbie podcasters can get discouraged, run out of ideas, or find that life is interfering with their pod dreams. Like a runner in a marathon, you must pace yourself and prepare for the long haul. Podcasting is not a sprint. You will need motivation and material to keep you going. At the outset, make an outline for the first few months of episodes so you'll have an idea of where you're going with your show and what you're shooting for. Even have some spare episodes in the queue, if possible, that you can publish if you have a week where you're feeling tired or downtrodden.

- **Plan your release schedule.** Podcasting is a no-rules endeavor (pretty much), so you get to decide how often you publish episodes. You can release episodes on a weekly or biweekly basis or all at once as a batch/season. Whatever you pick, do your best to be consistent about it. To build an audience, you have to let people know what your "store hours" are.

Specifics
Here are some odds and ends to keep in mind.

- **The why.** Decide what you're about. What is driving the show? Why is it important? We doubt that you are podcasting just to hear your own voice. You have something to say, and it's critical to convey it to the broadest audience possible. Write a mission statement for your show to keep you focused through the ups and downs.

- **What's in a name?** Romeo told Juliet that a rose by any other name would smell as sweet. Although this is true, names are decidedly important because they are part of the first impression you make. Your show's name gives your potential audience a clue to what you're about. (Remember Hilda's issues with her poorly named blogs?) But the truth is you can't even make that initial impression if people can't find you. So although a clever name is charming, a straightforward name will get you in the door quicker. And you also need to consider what feelings the title evokes.

For example, if you want to do a show that helps young moms manage their busy lives, you could call it *Calm Amidst the Chaos*. At first blush, the title scratches an itch and has some sweet alliteration. Although the word "mom" is not in the title, it could easily be in the description of the show. It's a decent choice for the target audience. On Apple's podcast site right now, the top parenting podcasts for moms have names that range from *Inspired to Action* to *At Home with Sally*. Few have the word "mom" in the title, but please note that those that do— *Mamalode* and *God-Centered Mom*, for example—pop up first.

I (Hilda) host a show called *Wise Traditions*. It's about food, farming, and the healing arts. While trying to come up with a name for the show, we went around and around in circles until we realized that it was the obvious choice. Although the title doesn't tell you that it's a health/nutrition show, it does communicate ancestral wisdom, which is foundational for the program. And the nonprofit organization that sponsors the show has an annual conference called Wise Traditions and a journal by the same name. In the end, we wondered what took us so long to settle on it. Another side benefit is that when you type the word "wise" into the search bar on many podcast apps, it is one of the first shows that appears.

So take some time picking out your name. And speaking of picking, feel free to pick your friends' and family's brains on this front. Use a poll on Facebook or find a focus group. Don't make this decision in a vacuum. But when push comes to shove, if the content is good, your audience will appreciate it, regardless of the name. Guess Romeo had it right all along.

> I *said*, "Follow me!"

Promotion
After you decide on the name for your show, get that name on every platform you can imagine. Reserve your domain name (for a future website) and your social media handles. It's optimal if they all match, of course. So going with the above example, if the show is called *Calm Amidst the Chaos,* you could buy the domain calmamidstthechaos.com and reserve the social media handles @catc on Twitter and Instagram and make a *Calm Amidst the Chaos* Facebook page, etc. The key is to have all the names reserved before the big unveiling of your show.

And then, use your social media accounts and website like crazy. Promote your show, engage with your audience, and make images/memes/graphics using Canva or PicMonkey. Get the word out there any way you can!

Artwork
I'm no Van Gogh (Charlie is the one who provided illustrations for this book, not Hilda) and chances are you're not an artist either. That's OK; you don't have to be. It is easy to find professionals these days—graphic artists or marketing experts can lend a hand in this arena. The best artwork to represent your show is simple, clear, neat, and readable as a thumbnail (because this is how it shows up on most apps and websites). It's OK to pay to have your artwork designed by a professional because it is usually affordable and looks better than if you drew it on your own.

Check out Fivrr and Upwork as a resource for help on this front.

And unless you're Oprah or some other big-name celebrity, we recommend leaving your photo out of the logo. Much like the name of
your show, the logo is part of the first impression you make with your
audience. A streamlined, clean, crisp look comes across better than a
picture of a stranger.

Branding (or rebranding)

A word of encouragement at this juncture: If you decide two years from
now that you want to change your name or artwork or what have you,
you can. Your brand is the part of your podcast that helps sell your
show to the world. But it's really the icing on the cake. It's not the most
important piece. What matters most is your content. So if at some point
you want to change your original brand/look, go for it. There might
be a cost in terms of time or money, but if you're doing an upgrade of
sorts, you will certainly gain listeners in the end so it should be worth
the chaos.

So take heart if you have any uncertainty at the start about some of
the above choices. You can begin again and even migrate your content
if/when you make such a move.

Media host

Before you dive into the podcasting world, you need to choose your
media host, which is a type of platform that launches your program to
where your audience awaits.

Think of it this way: If your show were a toy, you'd need to get it packaged and shipped out to stores. That's what the media hosts do. They
give your podcast an RSS (Really Simple Syndication) feed. The RSS
is your toy's shiny red case that allows your product to be placed on
the shelves of numerous "stores" (such as Apple Podcasts, Google Play,
iHeartRadio, YouTube, iVoox, etc.) where people can find and enjoy it.

There are many media hosts to choose from, including Libsyn, Blubrry,
PodBean, and Spreaker. I (Hilda) have used Libsyn and SoundCloud
(which might be out of business by the time this goes to print because

it is a free service). I recommend Libsyn because its hosting platform is very user-friendly. It has video tutorials and super-responsive customer service, should you ever get stuck. It can link your episode to a lot of destinations/"stores," including your Facebook page, your website, YouTube, and other podcast carriers such as Google Play.

Most media hosts offer very affordable packages (easily under $20 a month). It is worth the price. You can have a show without a hosting platform and simply post it on your website, but you will limit your reach. It's as if you only sold your toy on a local street corner. The only people who will ever listen to your show are those who visit your website. What you want to do is push your show out to a broader audience. The media host/hosting platform is like wheels for your show. It helps you branch out from your recording studio (or closet, as the case may be) to where the people are.

Once you choose a platform, simply follow its instructions (often video tutorials) for how to submit your episodes.

These companies can also help you navigate the world of the aforementioned "stores"—Apple Podcasts, Google Play, SoundCloud, TuneIn, iHeartRadio, YouTube, iVoox, Overcast, etc. Their job is to help you get your product out there, so they often make it super simple to do so. And all of them likely have help desks if you get stuck or overwhelmed.

Teamwork makes the dream work
You can launch alone, but you will not be able to sustain your show without help. Every idea begins with a person or two people in a garage with a dream. I'm thinking of Apple right now, but there are plenty of examples out there. Apple today is a huge machine that has fast-forwarded the technological advances of our age—from cell phones to TVs to virtual assistants in our homes that respond to our every whim. But the company is no longer run by two guys in a garage. Apple has thousands of employees.

What I'm getting at is that you are going to need to build a team to help you along the way. You will want to learn from those who have greater expertise than you do. You will want to find people who are passionate about your topic/show and invite them to team up with you. Here are some of the teams I've built (or joined) to help me pull off my show:

- I (Hilda) joined a local Meetup group (started by Charlie) that has helped me immeasurably. We've covered topics from editing to marketing to gear, and I have benefited from every single meeting I have attended. Although I am much more experienced now than I was at first, I still have much to learn. There is always someone in the room who knows more than I do about any given aspect of this medium. We offer each other mutual support and expertise in different fields, and we develop lifelong friendships.

- I designed an internship program and invite people to work with me for four to six months as volunteers. They can pick a specialty in areas that include social media support, guest scheduling, show note preparation, and technical assistance. Each person I have worked with has enjoyed the experience, and some have used it as a stepping-stone for their own careers. I have found that it's helpful to have them on board not only for their practical help, but also for the emotional encouragement they offer because they believe in the message and mission.

- I have networked with like-minded people in my field who are passionate about health/nutrition. They have offered invaluable support as well. So seek out people who love the topic of your show. As you bond, you will find out about events, retreats, and other gatherings where you can be encouraged and where you can showcase your podcast (in a subtle and socially acceptable way, of course).

6
Record:

Press That Red Button

Charlie

The basics of podcast recording are simple and no different from the recordings you might have first made on an iPhone, cassette, reel-to-reel, or even Super 8 (if anyone remembers that) device. For podcasts, the goal is to create consistent, clear sound. You do that by recording in a quiet environment with minimal background noise and by watching your volume levels on the mixer and your proximity to the microphone. Keeping you and your guest(s) equidistant from the mic is important. If they move their heads too far away, the listener will hear that. (Remember my first episode with three people and two microphones?) So do a little coaching with your hosts and guests about mic technique.

It is sometimes helpful to think about the flow of the content, and that can help with understanding the wiring. All those sounds go into the microphone, through the microphone cable, into the mixing board, and then out of the mixing board and into a digital recorder. You will listen to the show as you are getting ready to record so you can adjust the gain and level settings on the mixer to make it sound as even as possible.

Episode 0
Let's talk about what I like to call Episode 0. The most useful thing you can do is record a practice show and listen to it. It can be intimidating to push that red button, but don't worry—you can decide later if you will ever release it for public consumption. The goal is to get going. You will make a recording, do a quick edit, upload it, and then listen to it from a computer and/or a phone to test everything

before you do it with important material. When you are listening to a finished episode on a computer or phone, you learn a lot about your sound that you did not realize. When you listen as a listener would, you hear things differently. Listen to learn but not to criticize yourself. Use Episode 0 as a tool.

It might sound silly that you should listen to an uploaded version to get the full effect, but trust me, it's a helpful exercise. It's why a cook should sample the food that is being served. In another life, I helped run a restaurant on the Eastern Shore of Maryland. One day, we were trying out the steak, and it was awful. We asked the chef why it was so bad, and he admitted that he'd never eaten steak and had no idea if it tasted good or not. His soups were amazing, but his steaks were not.

You will never know what your show sounds like unless you listen to it coming out of a computer or phone, even if you might have a full setup and are able to listen with studio-quality monitors. Beyond listening to your voice and talking patterns, as I mentioned above, try to imagine how your listeners would listen and what might happen if they like the content. Will they check the notes? Do the notes have some relevant text—and hyperlinks? Will they know how to visit your website or follow you on social media?

"The difference between a podcaster and a savings bond is that one will mature."

Recording space: You might want to create a space where you podcast and make it special. Even if it is your bedroom, your closet (a great place acoustically!), or your car, a designated space will help put you in the correct frame of mind. For your in-studio guests, there is an important visual part you might want to spend a few moments developing. The appearance of your recording space can be vastly improved if you add a few simple visual clues. In our case, we have acoustic foam tiles over a portion of our office wall. It softens the overall sound and gets guests in the right frame of mind. You can do lots of things to make a space take on the guise of a special recording studio. In fact, during our first year, my wife saved hundreds of egg cartons that I considered using as sound proofing. (I didn't, but you can!)

Episode 0 has a few other things going for it, and I want to touch on them because they are important.

- It gives the host(s) a chance to hear their own verbal tics, the ones they did not know about (you know, like, ummmm).
- It gives you a chance to listen and think about your timing. Is it too long? Too short? Are you speaking too quickly?
- It gives you a chance to think about sponsors. You might not have one yet, but that should not stop you from thinking about where a sponsor spot could go.
- It gives you the opportunity to see how easy it is to listen to and/or download your podcast.

Episode 0 research: Write down five words that are relevant to your topic. You have now done all the research for Episode 0. The point is not to read from too many notes. You are having a conversation/interview, and the more animated the dialogue is, the more engaged your listener will be.

Getting ready

Start by setting the clock on your device. If you are using a digital recorder and have recently changed batteries or plugged it in without batteries, you want to set the clock. If you do not do this, you might be searching for your content in a folder where all the files have numbers for names and show up as having been recorded on the same date fifteen years ago. So, yeah, set the clock!

If your guest is a little nervous, find a way to help him or her relax. Getting the person to tell a relevant personal story is a great way to accomplish this. I have watched Hilda do this with guests on the *Wise Traditions* podcast many times. It allows the guest to have a positive warm-up, and if that story is retold after the recording starts, they will be ready to go and will deliver with confidence.

Go for it

Test all your gear and make a thirty-second sample. Here's how to do it.

- Plug a cable into the microphone and put the other end into one channel of the mixer. (And don't forget to turn the mixer on.)

- Plug a cable into one of the "line out" sources on the board (mine are RCA jacks that are clearly marked as "line out") and the other end *into* the digital recorder. I highlighted "into" because I have made the mistake of plugging my incoming content into the headphone jack, and that will not work.

- Plug your headphones into the digital recorder, *not* the mixer. You want to be monitoring what you are recording, and the output from the headphone jack on the board is not necessarily at the same volume as what is going into your recorder.

- Hit "record." Usually, but not always, this is a little red button.

- Make sure you are actually recording. Nothing is worse than finishing an interview and realizing that the recorder is stuck on "pause." I have done this at least once. It is not fun! So after you hit "record" and get in your first phrase or two, check the seconds counter. It should be increasing—it should not be a flashing zero.

- Talk and experiment with the gain, the track level, and the main mix level. Make a recording while you fade those settings so you can get used to adjusting all three of them to make the best sound.

- Hit "stop" and listen to what you just recorded.

Note on the aforementioned terms "gain" and "level": They both control the overall volume of your track. Think about it like water: The gain is the diameter of the pipe bringing you water, and the level is the knob on the tap. However, instead of only controlling the flow from the knob on the tap, you are also controlling the size of the pipe at the same time to make the best balance and get the best sound. Don't get tied up in knots about this. Just try fiddling with the knobs so you can see how they affect the sound.

Quick edit
Now that you have finished your first recording, you have a few more simple things to do.

"I'm tired of editing.
It's time for me to say, 'audios' to this episode!"

- Name the file right away.
  Do it immediately—before lunch or any kind of break. You will save yourself time in the long run.

- Save the file to the right location. This will create a backup of your raw data that will be easy to find when you are ready to edit.

A quick edit means you are not adding an intro or outro; you are just editing "raw" audio. This should take very little time. Do not take out the "ums" or "likes" or "you knows" at this point. Upload the file to your computer or to the software program you have downloaded for editing. If you want to, you can trim the beginning and the ending. By "trim," I simply mean "crop." Trimming or clipping is the same process you use when you crop an image in a photo app. You can cut out the part where you were getting everything ready to start and fumbling with the microphone or clearing your throat, and then you can cut out the extra silence at the end that is recorded when the speaking is done but the mics are still on. It's as simple as that.

Listen
Put your headphones on and give a listen.

What about editing?

Apart from the aforementioned trimming or clipping, we haven't talked much about editing because this is something you can outsource. If you want to do it yourself, however, it isn't hard. Editing a show is the same as editing a Word document. You highlight pieces you want to delete. You cut and paste segments you want elsewhere. A lot of editing software is very intuitive. Audacity (free download), GarageBand (comes with Apple products), and Audition (Adobe product) are probably the most commonly known and used. Talk to your peers in the podcasting community or tweet to us to get advice on what might be the best fit for you. Most people who do their own editing start with one of the free or inexpensive programs. Both GarageBand and Audacity have a wide range of capabilities and are excellent for podcasting.

One final editing tip: Whenever possible, try to do it immediately. You will remember everything better, you will be able to write the show notes in much greater detail, and you will be done!

7
Release:

Launch Your Show

Hilda

So you're ready to press "publish"? You want to get your message out to the world? Awesome! You were meant for this! You'll know you're ready for the starter pistol when you've 1) chosen your message and method, 2) gathered your gear, 3) built a little pre-buzz, 4) recorded Episode 0 and a handful more, 5) edited those episodes or handed them off to an editor, 6) added an introduction at the top and a tag at the end so people know what to expect when they start listening and where to find you when the show is over and maybe even thrown in some original (or free) music to spice things up. Now it's time to 7) release your show to the world.

"What do you mean 'publish'?"

The next thing you must do is pick a podcast media host/hosting platform. We mentioned earlier that you need to go with a company. See Chapter 5 for details on what those companies offer. Now is the time to pick one and get your .mp3 or .wav files submitted to your chosen platform so those files can be "packaged" and sent to "stores" for the audience to access.

I suggest getting your show in just one "store" to start with. (After all, this book is called *Podcasting Made Simple*.) Apple Podcasts is the most well-known, so I recommend starting there. It couldn't be easier. Just go to the podcast section of the iTunes store, and on the right-hand side of the page, you'll see the words "Submit a podcast."

Follow the step-by-step instructions and then hang tight. It can take two to three days for the approval process to kick in. Once you get the email message from Apple, you are good to go. Eventually, you can get in more "stores," and your show will gain steam. But for now, you are in the biggest distributor in the world. So promote the heck out of your amazing content and prepare to take on the world. You are rocking and rolling. You've got a podcast!

Afterword

We hope this book has demystified the podcasting process for you. It truly is a simple process, isn't it? If you don't have a show ready yet, hopefully you will soon.

It has been my (Hilda's) joy to introduce a lot of people to podcasting—from my organic hairdresser and my holistic dentist to young moms and wellness professionals. And I have a few more I am hoping to help launch this year as well. You might be surprised to learn that dentists and hairdressers have podcasts, but the truth is, everyone has a message to communicate that the world needs to hear. My hairdresser, Laura West of BellaWest Organic Salon in Alexandria, Virginia, wants to help stylists "go green" (for their health and the health of the Earth), and my dentist, Dr. Felix Liao, is eager to send the message that the health of our bodies is connected to the health (and shape) of our mouths. My point is: If they can do it, you can, too.

Please let me know if this book inspired you to launch your own show. I can be reached via Twitter (@holistichilda), Instagram (@holistic_hilda), or email (hilda@holistichilda.com). If you want a little more direction with your brand, goal-setting, or marketing (basically anything related to podcasting), reach out to me through my website, HolisticHilda.com. I offer free fifteen-minute consultations for beginners and podcast veterans alike. I can answer your questions and help you determine the next steps for making your podcast dreams come true. I also offer packages to help you take your show to the next level. So please take me up on any of the above!

In addition, Charlie offers hands-on technical assistance for podcasters. Go to the Podcast Village website (podcastvillage.com) to see his special offer for readers of this book.

Finally, we invite you to visit our Podcastingmadesimple.org website. We will continue to offer support for you as you take your show to the next level! There are articles and videos there with tips and tricks of the trade and a place for you to reach out to us with your questions. We are one big podern family now, so let's keep in touch!

www.ingramcontent.com/pod-product-compliance
Lightning Source LLC
Chambersburg PA
CBHW070817280326
41934CB00012B/3213